Stan and Vick

Written by Monica Hughes
Illustrated by Mike Byrne

Stan is not fit.

Stan can not grab Jack.

Vick gets Stan to jog up hills.

Vick gets Stan to run and
jump and twist.

Puff!

Vick fixes up a big canvas bag.

Vick gets Stan to box.

Stan boxes and boxes the
big canvas bag.

Stan did well.
Vick is glad.

Stan can grab Jack ...

... and Vick can help!